# APPLE INTELLIGENCE
## An Honest Review – Hype or Reality?

*What's Coming, What's Missing, and How
It Will Transform the Tech Landscape*

**J. Andy Peters**

# Table of Contents

# Introduction

The tech world buzzed with anticipation as Apple, known for its innovation and perfectionist ethos, made a bold claim about the future of its products. With whispers of *Apple Intelligence* echoing across the industry, it seemed as though the company was preparing to unveil something revolutionary. At WWDC 2024, Apple's keynote promised a new era for its devices, one where artificial intelligence would fundamentally change how users interacted with their iPhones, Macs, iPads, and even the Vision Pro. For months leading up to that moment, the world was on edge, wondering: Could Apple, the most valuable tech company in the world, truly unlock the full potential of AI in a way no one else had?

Since then, however, the dust hasn't settled quite as expected. The once-exciting promise of Apple's AI integration seems to be taking longer to materialize than anticipated. The grand announcement, a bold leap into the future, has yet to live up to its original hype. While the devices themselves have continued to evolve with each new release, the seamless, futuristic experience that Apple promised—one that would redefine tech as we know it—has remained elusive.

This book aims to explore and unpack *Apple Intelligence*—what it is, what's been delivered, and what's still on the horizon. From the AI-powered tools that were first teased to the slower-than-expected rollouts, the goal here is to dive deep into what Apple is really offering its users, examining how these new AI features work in practice, and whether they meet the lofty expectations set by the company itself. We will assess whether Apple is truly on the verge of something groundbreaking or if, like many tech promises before it, this one will fade into the background of unfulfilled potential. By breaking down the elements of this new AI integration across Apple's platforms, this book will provide you with a comprehensive, honest, and no-holds-barred review of Apple Intelligence.

# Chapter 1: The Apple Intelligence Promise – What We Were Told

In June 2024, all eyes were on Apple as they took the stage at their Worldwide Developers Conference (WWDC). Every year, the tech giant uses this platform to unveil new products, software updates, and innovations that set the tone for the future of their ecosystem. But this year, the spotlight was particularly intense. Apple had promised that this would be the most important WWDC in years, and with the growing buzz surrounding AI, the anticipation was palpable. The question on everyone's mind was: *What does Apple have in store for artificial intelligence, and how will it reshape their entire product lineup?*

When Apple's senior leadership took the stage, the answer came loud and clear. With the launch of *Apple Intelligence*, the company unveiled their vision of an AI-driven future, promising an entirely new experience across their devices. For the first time, Apple was positioning itself as a leader in the rapidly evolving world of artificial intelligence, committing to integrate AI features into their flagship products in a way that would not only enhance usability but also transform how people interacted with their devices.

The announcement was big, and it was clear that Apple was going all-in. The keynote promised smarter devices, more intuitive interactions, and deeper integrations with AI at every level of the Apple ecosystem. The iPhone, iPad, Mac, and even the Vision Pro were all set to receive AI upgrades that would improve everything from writing and communication tools to predictive capabilities, personal assistants, and machine learning-driven optimizations.

In particular, Apple presented a new suite of AI-powered features, including *Apple's Writing Tools*, which promised to revolutionize how users would create content, from generating text to enhancing written communication in a way that felt personalized and natural. The integration of AI into apps, system-wide features, and even hardware was set to make each device smarter, learning more about users over time to anticipate needs, improve productivity, and enhance the overall experience.

Apple's approach seemed unique. Instead of simply following the path carved by other tech giants like Google or Microsoft, they proposed something more refined: an AI system that would seamlessly integrate into the user's daily life without feeling intrusive or overwhelming. The promise was clear—Apple Intelligence would be intelligent enough to learn from user behavior, predictive enough to offer relevant suggestions, and adaptive enough to feel like a personal assistant on every device.

For those watching the announcement, it was clear: Apple wasn't just dipping its toes into the world of AI. It was ready to stake its claim, positioning itself as the company that could take AI beyond a buzzword and integrate it into the very fabric of its ecosystem. It was an ambitious, forward-looking vision, one that seemed poised to usher in a new era of technology. But like any big promise, it raised just as many questions as it answered. Would Apple's AI be the game-changer they claimed it would be? Or was it just another shiny new feature that would take years to fully materialize? Only time would tell.

When Apple took the wraps off *Apple Intelligence*, it was clear they weren't simply introducing a new set of AI tools—they were promising a transformative leap in how we interact with technology. Apple's pitch was bold and filled with the kind of visionary language that has always defined the company's ethos. For years, Apple had been refining its hardware and software ecosystems, creating a seamless user experience across devices. Now, with *Apple Intelligence*, the company was attempting to take that harmony to the next level, seamlessly integrating AI into every aspect of the Apple experience.

The key vision Apple sold to the world was one of "personalization at scale." They wanted to make their devices smarter, more intuitive, and deeply integrated into users' daily lives. The pitch was that these AI features would evolve alongside the user, adapting to individual preferences, habits, and workflows. With the power of machine learning, Apple Intelligence would allow devices to anticipate what users wanted to do next, offer smart suggestions, and even help craft content in ways that felt uniquely tailored to each individual.

One of the most significant features announced was *AI-powered writing tools*, which were described as being able to transform how users interacted with text. From drafting emails to creating entire documents, these writing tools were set to not only assist in grammar and syntax but also make more context-driven suggestions—helping users refine tone, style, and structure based on the intended audience or purpose. The promise was that these tools would go beyond simple text completion or correction; they would evolve to understand the user's writing style and preferences, offering more personalized suggestions as the system learned over time.

In addition to writing, Apple's AI-powered personal assistants were slated to be a major focus. Siri, Apple's long-standing voice assistant, had always been an integral part of the Apple ecosystem, but it was often seen as a step behind compared to rivals like Amazon's Alexa or Google Assistant. With Apple Intelligence, however, Siri was set to get a major upgrade. The new Siri, enhanced by Apple's AI, promised to be not just more accurate but more anticipatory. It was designed to integrate seamlessly across all Apple devices—iPhones, Macs, iPads, and even the Vision Pro—allowing users to control their devices with ease, while also offering intelligent suggestions and performing tasks more efficiently. Whether scheduling meetings, suggesting apps, or answering questions, Siri was positioned to become a more proactive assistant, understanding context in a deeper way and offering helpful, personalized insights in real time.

Alongside Siri, Apple also unveiled an expanded set of predictive capabilities. These weren't just about predicting what you might want to do next, but about anticipating the kinds of tasks that would help improve productivity. For instance, your iPhone could predict the right time to send a message, suggest a contact you might want to call, or recommend a news article based on your interests and recent browsing habits. With machine learning algorithms constantly running in the background, Apple promised that their devices would become more aware of what was important to you and how they could assist in your daily life.

For the Vision Pro, Apple's most futuristic product, the integration of AI was even more ambitious. The Vision Pro headset was designed to offer an entirely new way of interacting with digital content, combining augmented reality (AR) and virtual reality (VR). AI was set to play a key role in making this experience seamless and intuitive. By leveraging the power of Apple Intelligence, Vision Pro would adapt to the user's environment, understanding spatial context, and delivering personalized content—whether for work, entertainment, or education. The idea was that users would no longer be passive consumers of digital content but would actively engage with a world that felt uniquely tailored to their needs.

Apple's vision was clear: AI would not just enhance the way users interact with their devices; it would change the very fabric of the Apple ecosystem, making each device smarter, more intuitive, and more deeply integrated into the user's life. From writing to productivity, personal assistance to virtual reality, Apple promised that its AI features would deliver an experience that was both innovative and essential—revolutionizing the user experience across the entire lineup of Apple products.

## Chapter 2: The Reality of Apple Intelligence – What's Available Now?

The rollout of *Apple Intelligence* has been much more gradual than the initial hype suggested, leaving many eager users waiting patiently for the promise of a fully integrated AI experience. While the excitement surrounding Apple's announcement at WWDC 2024 had set high expectations, the company chose to release features piece by piece, making sure each update was thoroughly tested and refined before reaching the masses. This step-by-step rollout allowed Apple to fine-tune the AI tools and ensure that they would live up to their claims.

The first major milestone came with the release of the latest iPhone model in September 2024. While this new iPhone was highly anticipated, it arrived without any of the AI-powered features that had been promised during the WWDC keynote. Instead, users found the device to be a polished iteration of the previous model, boasting improved hardware, a faster processor, and enhanced camera features. The absence of the *Apple Intelligence* features was a surprising omission, especially given the buzz surrounding them just a few months earlier.

However, Apple was quick to address this gap. A few weeks after the iPhone launch, the company began rolling out a series of software updates aimed at integrating the first wave of AI features across its product lineup. These updates were delivered via the iOS 17.1 and macOS updates, marking the beginning of the AI-enhanced experience Apple had promised. For many users, this marked the first taste of *Apple Intelligence*—and the first opportunity to see how these features would perform in real-world conditions.

The initial software updates focused primarily on smaller, more incremental changes to existing features, like improved Siri functionality and the introduction of more context-aware notifications. While these updates were a welcome addition, they fell short of the grand promises made during the

WWDC keynote. The AI-powered writing tools, which had generated the most excitement, were notably absent, leaving many users wondering when they would see the promised generative AI capabilities in action.

By the end of 2024, Apple began pushing out updates that introduced the first fully integrated *Apple Intelligence* features. These updates, which were rolled out to iPhones, iPads, and Macs, included the much-anticipated writing tools. Users were now able to try out AI-assisted writing, with the ability to compose emails, messages, and documents using Apple's new generative AI system. The AI would analyze the text in real-time, suggesting improvements to grammar, tone, and even structure. For many, this was the first real taste of the promise Apple had made: a smarter, more intuitive device that could help craft content in a way that felt personalized and natural.

In 2025, Apple plans to complete the rollout of *Apple Intelligence* with further updates to iOS, macOS, and iPadOS. By then, more advanced features are expected to be fully integrated, including AI-driven predictive capabilities that will anticipate user needs, smarter personal assistants, and deeper AI tools for content creation. The Vision Pro, Apple's next-generation mixed-reality headset, is also expected to receive a significant update in early 2025, with AI features that will push the boundaries of augmented reality.

However, despite the ongoing updates and gradual rollout, many users continue to feel a sense of impatience. With each software update, the promise of *Apple Intelligence* feels like it's just within reach—but never quite fully realized. The timeline is ambitious, and while Apple has certainly made progress, there's still a long way to go before the full vision of an AI-driven ecosystem becomes a reality for all users.

When Apple finally began rolling out its highly anticipated *Apple Intelligence* features, the focus was initially on the generative AI writing tools. This was one of the most talked-about elements during the WWDC keynote, and for good reason. Apple positioned these tools as revolutionary, designed to not only assist in creating content but to completely change how users interact with text across its ecosystem.

The generative AI writing tools, which were first introduced in the iOS 17.1 and macOS updates, promised to do more than simple text editing. They were meant to assist users in drafting emails, creating documents, and even generating ideas or outlines from scratch. The idea was that these tools would integrate smoothly with Apple's native apps like Notes, Mail, and Pages, providing contextual assistance and personalized suggestions based on a user's writing style and needs.

When users first got their hands on these tools, there was both excitement and frustration. The initial version of the writing tools worked well for basic tasks like suggesting grammar fixes and rewording awkward sentences. For example, users could highlight a portion of their text and ask the AI to "rewrite" it in a more formal tone or to provide a more concise version of a lengthy paragraph. The AI was able to generate helpful suggestions that were often spot-on and useful for improving the clarity or tone of a document. In many ways, the generative capabilities of Apple's writing tools were on par with what was offered by other AI-powered writing assistants like Grammarly or Microsoft's Word Copilot.

However, the feature was far from perfect. Many users quickly noticed that while the AI could help with simple corrections and suggestions, it struggled when it came to more complex writing tasks. The writing tools had a tendency to generate repetitive or overly generic suggestions, especially in longer pieces of text. For instance, when users asked the AI to rewrite an entire paragraph or provide alternative ways of phrasing a particular sentence, the results often felt mechanical or lacking in originality. Some users also noted that the writing tools would sometimes suggest changes that didn't quite fit the context, leading to awkward or unintentionally funny results.

Another major point of frustration was the interface. Apple's design philosophy has always been centered around simplicity and ease of use, but with the writing tools, some users found the experience to be unintuitive. The process of accessing the tools was more cumbersome than expected. To use the writing tools, users had to highlight their text, open a menu, and select from a range of options. But this wasn't the only issue—the menu itself was somewhat redundant. For example, one could select a feature like "Rewrite" directly from the toolbar, or use another button labeled "Show Writing Tools," which opened a list of the same options again. This repetitive UI caused confusion and led to a disjointed experience that didn't align with Apple's typical streamlined design ethos.

As for the AI's predictive capabilities, while the system worked well in some instances, it often fell short when it came to more nuanced or creative tasks. For example, users might ask for help generating an email reply based on a series of recent messages, but the AI often failed to pick up on subtleties in tone or missed key context. While it was an efficient tool for generating basic text, the AI seemed to lack the deeper understanding that would make it a true collaborator for content creation.

Along with the writing tools, Apple also began rolling out other AI-powered features, such as enhanced personal assistants, smarter Siri, and predictive notifications. Siri, for example, could now better understand contextual commands and anticipate what a user might need next. A request like "Hey Siri, book me a flight" could now trigger not just the booking process but also ask follow-up questions, like preferred times or airline choices, based on the user's past behavior. While Siri's performance improved, many users still found that it fell short of the capabilities offered by its competitors, like Amazon's Alexa or Google Assistant.

One notable limitation that became apparent as the *Apple Intelligence* features were rolled out was the absence of any significant AI integration in the Vision Pro. Despite the Vision Pro being Apple's most futuristic platform, the device didn't receive the same level of AI enhancements that other devices did. This was a curious omission, as many had expected Apple to leverage the Vision Pro's advanced hardware and immersive capabilities to introduce next-generation AI experiences. Without the promised AI features, the Vision Pro felt more like an expensive, albeit impressive, piece of hardware rather than a transformative, AI-powered platform.

In terms of the other features, there were also limitations. While the AI was certainly helpful in some instances, it didn't yet live up to the hype surrounding Apple's claims of revolutionizing user experiences. Many users were hoping for an all-encompassing, unified AI experience, where everything from writing tools to personal assistants worked together in perfect harmony. Instead, they found that each AI feature felt isolated, with little integration between them. This lack of cohesion was one of the major criticisms from users, as it seemed as though Apple had introduced a collection of promising tools that didn't yet live up to their full potential.

In summary, while Apple's generative AI tools and other *Apple Intelligence* features showed promise, their rollout was imperfect. There were areas of real potential, especially in terms of simplifying tasks and providing more personalized user experiences, but the execution still had a long way to go. As with many early tech rollouts, the first wave of AI features felt like a work in progress—offering glimpses of what could be, but not yet delivering on the grand vision that Apple had pitched.

Despite the promising start and gradual rollout of *Apple Intelligence*, several key features that were initially promised have yet to materialize, leaving users wondering when, or if, they will ever arrive. The gaps in Apple's AI rollout have become increasingly apparent, as some of the most highly anticipated features remain conspicuously absent. Among the most notable missing elements are the full integration of *Apple Intelligence* into the Vision Pro, as well as the refinement of predictive tools that were promised to make Apple devices smarter and more intuitive.

One of the biggest disappointments for many users has been the lack of *Apple Intelligence* in the Vision Pro, Apple's flagship augmented reality (AR) headset. Despite being one of the company's most futuristic products, the Vision Pro has yet to see any substantial AI integration. While Apple has included some basic AI features, like facial recognition and object tracking, the deeper integration of machine learning and AI tools that was promised remains absent. Vision Pro users, many of whom had eagerly awaited AI-driven enhancements that would elevate the AR experience, are left wondering when—and if—the immersive headset will fully benefit from *Apple Intelligence*'s capabilities.

At the time of writing, the Vision Pro remains largely reliant on traditional interaction models, without the robust, AI-powered tools that have been introduced on other Apple devices. The promised features, such as context-aware assistants and AI-driven content generation within the headset's interface, have yet to materialize. For users who were hoping that the Vision Pro would set a new standard for AR experiences, this lack of AI integration feels like a missed opportunity, and a glaring gap in Apple's strategy.

Another area where users have expressed frustration is with the *predictive tools* that Apple touted during the initial announcement. These tools were meant to anticipate users' needs and suggest actions based on patterns, such as predicting the next app a user might open, or even drafting responses to emails based on the tone and content of the conversation. While some of these predictive features have been partially rolled out—like the ability to suggest calendar events based on email content or location-based reminders—they are still in their infancy and often lack the sophistication that many users were expecting.

For instance, Apple's version of predictive text, which was meant to generate contextually relevant suggestions for everything from emails to notes, often falls short of the seamless experience promised during WWDC 2024. Users report that the suggestions can sometimes feel irrelevant or out of place, leading to a more fragmented experience rather than the smooth, predictive flow Apple had envisioned. Furthermore, the ability to "learn" from users' behavior and adapt accordingly remains somewhat inconsistent.

Even more concerning is the lack of full integration across Apple's product ecosystem. While features like Siri's voice assistant have received some improvements, such as smarter responses and deeper integration with Apple services, they still fall short of the level of intelligence users were hoping for. In a world where Alexa, Google Assistant, and other AI assistants continue to evolve rapidly, Apple's Siri feels stagnant in comparison. Users are still waiting for the day when Siri can truly predict their needs—offering recommendations, managing tasks, and controlling their environment with the same level of sophistication as other leading AI assistants.

The absence of full-scale integration across Apple's various platforms is another point of contention. While users have seen some advancements in iOS, macOS, and iPadOS, the promise that these devices would work in unison, with AI tools seamlessly communicating between platforms, has not fully come to fruition. For example, while the new writing tools are available on Macs and iPads, they don't yet translate seamlessly across devices. A user might be editing a document on their MacBook with the AI-powered writing tool, but when they switch to their iPhone, the experience feels disjointed, and the same tools are often not available or less effective. This lack of cross-device synergy is a major limitation of the current rollout.

As Apple continues to work on refining and expanding *Apple Intelligence*, it's clear that many users are still left waiting for the complete, integrated experience that was promised. While the company has made notable strides with features like AI-powered writing tools, smarter personal assistants, and predictive suggestions, there is still much to be done. With the full potential of *Apple Intelligence* still on the horizon, many are left wondering whether Apple can deliver on its ambitious vision in the coming months—or if these gaps will remain for the foreseeable future.

## Chapter 3: Delays, Missed Promises, and the Road Ahead

The delay in the full rollout of *Apple Intelligence* has been one of the most talked-about aspects of this ambitious project. When Apple first announced their AI-driven initiative at WWDC 2024, the tech community expected a swift implementation across all their devices. However, as the months passed, it became clear that the promised AI features were not arriving as quickly as many had anticipated. The initial timeline suggested that much of the functionality would be available by the end of 2024, but Apple later revised the schedule, stating that all *Apple Intelligence* features would be fully integrated by March 2025. This extended timeline has left many users wondering why the rollout is taking so much longer than expected.

The delays have sparked a range of reactions, from impatience to skepticism, and while Apple has remained relatively tight-lipped about the specifics, there are a few potential reasons behind the extended timeline. Technically, developing AI systems that integrate seamlessly across Apple's vast ecosystem of devices is a massive undertaking. Apple's approach to AI, unlike that of some other tech giants, focuses heavily on user privacy and local processing rather than relying on cloud-based models. This approach undoubtedly adds a layer of complexity to the AI development process, as it requires building systems that can process data in real-time on the device itself, without sending user information to external servers. While this focus on privacy is a major selling point for Apple, it also means that every new AI feature must be meticulously tested to ensure both functionality and security.

Moreover, Apple's commitment to delivering a high-quality, user-friendly experience could also be a factor in the delays. Unlike some other companies that may rush out AI tools with limited functionality, Apple is known for its attention to detail. The company's typical approach is to introduce new features gradually, allowing time for feedback and fine-tuning before rolling them out to the broader user base. While this cautious strategy helps avoid the problems that often arise from premature product releases, it can also mean longer waiting times for users eager to experience the full promise of *Apple Intelligence*.

Strategically, Apple may also be delaying the full rollout in order to avoid the pitfalls of launching incomplete or underdeveloped features. The tech industry is filled with examples of companies rushing to release new technologies, only to face criticism when they fail to meet user expectations. By spacing out the rollout of *Apple Intelligence*, Apple is likely aiming to build a more stable foundation and avoid a repeat of past mistakes. This careful, step-by-step approach allows the company to gather user feedback, identify potential issues, and make necessary adjustments before fully committing to the next phase of AI integration.

Another potential reason for the delay could be the need to refine the integration of *Apple Intelligence* across Apple's diverse product lineup. Apple's ecosystem is vast, with a wide array of devices ranging from iPhones and iPads to Macs, the Apple Watch, and the Vision Pro. Each of these devices has its own unique hardware and software requirements, which means that integrating AI across the entire ecosystem is no small feat. The challenge lies not only in ensuring that each device functions optimally with *Apple Intelligence* but also in creating a seamless experience for users who switch between devices on a daily basis. Getting this integration right takes time and testing—time that Apple is clearly willing to invest to ensure a polished product.

Despite the delays, Apple's promise that all features will be complete by March 2025 sets an important milestone. It shows that the company is committed to getting things right, even if that means a longer wait. For now, users are left to navigate the evolving landscape of *Apple Intelligence*, eagerly awaiting the day when the full vision Apple has promised will come to life. While the extended timeline has been frustrating for some, the eventual payoff could be worth the wait, offering a more refined and polished AI experience that aligns with Apple's reputation for excellence.

As the clock ticks down toward March 2025, Apple enthusiasts and critics alike are eagerly speculating about what will finally be delivered in the next round of updates. The anticipation has only grown as Apple continues to hint at the future of *Apple Intelligence*. With several promised features still in the pipeline, the upcoming updates have the potential to either solidify Apple's position as an AI leader or risk leaving users disappointed by yet another round of incremental improvements.

One of the most eagerly awaited updates is the full integration of *Apple Intelligence* across the Vision Pro. Apple has hinted that the Vision Pro will finally benefit from the deep AI integration that was promised back in 2024, offering an immersive AR experience powered by machine learning, predictive tools, and content creation capabilities. These AI-driven features are expected to enable the Vision Pro to learn from users' preferences and anticipate actions, creating a truly intuitive interaction model. The promise is that by 2025, the Vision Pro will evolve from being a high-tech curiosity into a fully-fledged tool that can be used seamlessly in both work and play, unlocking new potentials for AR that Apple's competitors have yet to explore.

In addition to the Vision Pro, Apple is expected to refine its generative AI writing tools. Based on the feedback received from users, it's clear that while the tools work well for basic text editing, there is still much room for improvement. The upcoming updates will likely focus on enhancing the AI's ability to generate more contextually relevant suggestions, make creative leaps in content creation, and offer a more personalized experience based on the user's writing style. One potential breakthrough could be the integration of these tools across more applications, not just in text-heavy apps like Pages or Mail but in photo and video editing software, as well. Imagine an AI that can assist with both written content and media creation, adjusting captions, generating storylines, or even helping with scriptwriting for video content.

Another area of potential growth is Apple's predictive capabilities. The next set of updates may include more advanced machine learning algorithms capable of anticipating users' needs with greater precision. For example, the AI might learn when to push notifications, suggest apps based on location, or even pre-load apps that the user typically needs at certain times of the day. Apple's goal is to create a truly anticipatory user experience, where devices can act before the user even asks for something. This would represent a leap beyond today's reactive AI systems and truly showcase Apple's ambition to create a smarter, more personalized experience for its users.

Yet, there are still significant hurdles Apple needs to overcome if these features are going to live up to the hype. The AI tools will need to be fine-tuned to avoid the repetitiveness and occasional awkwardness that users have reported in early tests. Additionally, many are watching closely to see if Apple can maintain its commitment to privacy while rolling out more sophisticated AI tools. Will the company be able to balance robust, predictive capabilities with its stringent privacy policies, or will it risk user trust in an effort to push out more advanced AI features?

In some ways, the updates expected in 2025 could be a make-or-break moment for *Apple Intelligence*. While Apple has delivered some solid tools, the coming features will be crucial in determining whether the company can truly revolutionize the AI landscape or if it will simply fall behind as its competitors—who are already far ahead in AI development—continue to innovate at a rapid pace. Whether these next updates will truly transform the user experience or merely serve as incremental improvements to an already well-established ecosystem remains to be seen. The next chapter in Apple's AI journey will be defined not only by what is delivered but by how well it meets the ambitious promises made at WWDC 2024.

## Chapter 4: The Tech Landscape – How Apple Intelligence Fits In

As Apple rolls out its *Apple Intelligence* features, the company's efforts are under intense scrutiny, not just from its loyal user base but also from the broader tech industry. The world of artificial intelligence is rapidly evolving, and Apple's rivals—most notably Google and Microsoft—have been aggressive in their AI pursuits for several years. As these companies continue to push the envelope in AI innovation, Apple is left with a crucial question: Is it setting the pace in this race, or is it simply catching up with the industry giants?

## Apple vs. Google

Google has long been at the forefront of AI, with its vast infrastructure and data-driven approach to machine learning. The company has invested heavily in AI, particularly through its Google Brain project, and has integrated cutting-edge AI capabilities across its suite of services, from Google

Search and Assistant to its cloud-based AI tools. Google's Android ecosystem, combined with the massive amount of data the company collects from users worldwide, allows them to offer highly personalized experiences that Apple has not yet matched. In addition, Google's generative AI tools, such as Bard and Google Docs' AI-powered writing assistance, have set a high bar for what users expect in terms of creativity and efficiency.

While Apple's *Apple Intelligence* is promising, its approach is quite different from Google's. Apple has consistently prioritized privacy and security, which means it doesn't rely on the same kind of data collection practices that Google uses to fuel its AI. This strategy has its merits, particularly in terms of user trust, but it also limits Apple's ability to develop AI as quickly and as extensively as its competitors. Google's AI systems benefit from vast amounts of real-time data, giving them a significant advantage when it comes to personalization and predictive capabilities. In contrast, Apple's AI tools are more restrained, especially with their focus on on-device processing rather than relying on cloud-based models. While Apple's privacy-first approach is a key differentiator, it may hinder the company's ability to offer the same breadth of AI services that Google provides.

## Apple vs. Microsoft

Microsoft is another key player in the AI space, having made significant strides through its integration of OpenAI's GPT technology into its suite of tools, including Word, Excel, and Teams. The company's approach to AI has been expansive, blending cutting-edge language models with enterprise-grade software to create AI-enhanced tools that assist both individuals and businesses. The success of Microsoft Copilot, which integrates generative AI directly into productivity software, has positioned the company as a leader in the AI-powered workplace.

Apple's AI tools, particularly the writing assistants, have yet to fully catch up with Microsoft's offerings. While Apple's writing tools are capable and useful, they are still in the early stages of development, offering a more basic set of functionalities compared to Microsoft's generative AI features. Microsoft's use of OpenAI's GPT models in their products allows them to provide a level of sophistication and versatility in their AI tools that Apple's more rudimentary offerings can't match—at least not yet. However, Apple does have a unique advantage in the consumer market. Where Microsoft's AI is largely focused on the business and productivity sectors, Apple's *Apple Intelligence* promises to enhance a wide range of consumer experiences, from content creation to entertainment and personal productivity.

## Apple vs. Amazon

Amazon, another major competitor, has made AI a cornerstone of its strategy, particularly through its voice assistant, Alexa. Alexa's ability to seamlessly integrate with smart home devices has positioned Amazon as a leader in AI for the home. However, where Amazon truly shines is in its cloud computing services through AWS, which has allowed it to offer AI services to developers and businesses, fueling the broader AI ecosystem.

Apple, on the other hand, has been slower to embrace the smart home space with the same intensity as Amazon, and *Apple Intelligence* has yet to offer the kind of deep, AI-powered integrations that Alexa and other Amazon products boast. The Vision Pro, for example, may eventually offer some smart home capabilities, but it's not yet clear how *Apple Intelligence* will compete with Amazon's ecosystem in terms of voice assistance or IoT (Internet of Things) functionality. Still, Apple's focus on privacy and seamless integration within its own ecosystem may offer it a unique position that Amazon's Alexa, which is more dependent on cloud services, cannot fully replicate.

## Differentiation or Catching Up?

The question that looms over Apple's AI strategy is whether it's truly innovating or simply playing catch-up. While Apple has certainly made strides with its *Apple Intelligence* rollout, the company is not leading the AI race in the same way it has in other areas. Apple's focus on privacy, while laudable, has resulted in a slower and more cautious approach to AI development. In contrast, companies like Google, Microsoft, and Amazon have aggressively pursued AI innovation, integrating it deeply into their services and products. Google and Microsoft, in particular, have launched sophisticated generative AI tools that are already changing how people work, create, and interact with technology.

However, Apple's approach to AI is not without merit. The company is uniquely positioned to leverage its hardware-software ecosystem, allowing it to create AI tools that work seamlessly across its devices. *Apple Intelligence* is built to enhance the user experience in ways that feel organic and natural within the Apple ecosystem—whether that's through smarter devices or AI-powered productivity tools. Apple's incremental approach, while slower, may allow it to deliver a more polished and user-friendly AI experience once the full suite of features is available. By focusing on delivering high-quality, user-centered AI that prioritizes security and privacy, Apple is carving out a niche that could resonate with users who value these principles over the raw power of data-driven AI.

In the end, while Apple may not be leading the charge in AI the way Google and Microsoft are, it is certainly not out of the race. The company's focus on refining its AI offerings and ensuring they integrate smoothly with its hardware could allow it to catch up quickly in the coming years. Whether Apple's AI tools can eventually match or surpass the sophistication of its competitors remains to be seen, but one thing is clear: Apple is in this for the long haul, and it has the resources and the brand loyalty to make its AI vision a reality.

Apple's user experience philosophy has always been a driving force behind its success, but when it comes to the integration of artificial intelligence, this commitment to simplicity and accessibility creates both advantages and challenges. Apple has always prided itself on creating devices that just work—products that, upon first use, feel intuitive and familiar, even to those who aren't particularly tech-savvy. This user-centric approach is central to how Apple develops its features, including the ambitious *Apple Intelligence* suite. While this philosophy aims to make AI tools more accessible and seamless, it can sometimes lead to a restrictive experience for users who want more customization or control.

Apple's focus is clear: the company wants its AI to feel natural and unobtrusive. Whether it's generative tools for writing, predictive assistants, or context-aware features, the goal is for these tools to enhance the user experience without overwhelming it. This means that, typically, Apple's AI features are built into the ecosystem in a way that doesn't require users to dive into complex settings or figure out how to "optimize" the experience. Users are presented with a polished, streamlined interface, where AI works silently in the background to make suggestions, anticipate needs, or automate tasks without calling attention to itself. For example, Siri can quickly set reminders or send messages, while the generative writing tools can refine an email draft with minimal input from the user. It's a system that feels like it's there to assist rather than complicate.

However, this very simplicity can also be a limiting factor. Apple's tendency to control how features are used—whether it's AI-powered writing tools or Siri's predictive capabilities—means that there's often less room for customization. Apple doesn't allow the same level of user input or configuration that some other tech companies might. For instance, Google's Assistant and Microsoft's AI tools offer more flexibility in how users can modify their preferences or control the AI's behavior. Google's approach allows users to dive deeper into settings, adjust the AI's tone, and fine-tune the experience to their liking. By comparison, Apple tends to keep things minimal, which is great for beginners or those who don't want to think too much about how the AI works, but it leaves advanced users wanting more control.

In addition to this, Apple's approach to privacy significantly shapes how its AI tools operate. Apple has long distinguished itself from other tech giants by placing a strong emphasis on user privacy. While companies like Google and Microsoft thrive on collecting data to fuel their AI and improve their services, Apple has remained steadfast in its commitment to local processing, which keeps much of the data on users' devices rather than sending it to the cloud. This focus on privacy means that Apple's AI can't benefit from the same vast troves of personal data that other companies use to improve their models and offer more personalized experiences.

For example, Google's AI tools are able to make highly accurate predictions and offer personalized recommendations because they have access to a wealth of user data—search history, location tracking, purchase habits, and more. Apple, on the other hand, collects far less data in this way, and while this makes its products more private, it also limits the extent to which Apple's AI can "learn" from user behaviors. This trade-off—privacy versus personalization—creates a fundamental difference in how Apple's AI evolves compared to its competitors. While users of Google's AI may get suggestions that feel incredibly specific to their needs, Apple users benefit from a heightened sense of security, knowing that their data is being processed securely and privately, rather than being stored or analyzed by remote servers.

In the long run, Apple's stance on privacy could help set it apart from competitors. As data privacy continues to be a growing concern, particularly in the wake of various scandals involving user data misuse, Apple's insistence on keeping data on-device could be a major selling point. However, this philosophy also means that Apple's AI may not be as powerful or as fast to adapt as that of companies like Google, who have the advantage of vast amounts of user data to train their models. The trade-off is clear: Apple's AI might not be as finely tuned or predictive, but it offers a more secure and private experience. Whether this balance will help Apple's AI catch up with, or surpass, its competitors remains to be seen.

# Chapter 5: Criticism, Doubts, and the Apple Ecosystem

When Apple first introduced the concept of *Apple Intelligence*, it created significant excitement among its user base. The promise of AI-driven tools—tools that could not only assist with everyday tasks but also revolutionize the way users interacted with their devices—was a major talking point at WWDC 2024. The buzz surrounding these advancements suggested a future where Apple devices would be even more intuitive, more predictive, and more intelligent. Users were eager for seamless, powerful AI features that could make their daily lives easier, from smarter personal assistants to creative tools that could help generate content with minimal effort. But as the rollout of *Apple Intelligence* unfolded, there was a noticeable gap between expectations and reality.

One of the main challenges has been that many of the features users were most excited about, such as advanced predictive capabilities and fully integrated generative AI tools, have either been delayed or arrived with limited functionality. For example, while Apple's generative writing tools did offer some help in streamlining tasks like editing and rewording, they didn't quite live up to the high expectations set during the initial announcements. Users who anticipated a more creative, expansive AI—one that could autonomously create text, come up with new ideas, or fully adapt to their personal writing style—were often left underwhelmed by the early iterations. The tools worked for basic tasks but fell short when it came to the more complex needs of power users or those looking for deeper customization.

Moreover, the lack of immediate, full integration into all of Apple's product lines—especially the Vision Pro, which many hoped would be a standout showcase for *Apple Intelligence*—has left some users feeling disappointed. While Apple promised a transformative experience with AI across its ecosystem, the delayed rollout, with features still not fully available, has created a sense of frustration among those who expected the company to hit the ground running. Apple's decision to take a more cautious approach, rolling out AI tools gradually, may have been aimed at ensuring quality and stability, but for users eager to experience the full range of *Apple Intelligence*, this slow pace has been a letdown.

Apple's "closed ecosystem" philosophy is both a boon and a burden when it comes to AI innovation. On one hand, it allows Apple to maintain tight control over the user experience, ensuring that all AI features work seamlessly across its devices. The integration between hardware and software in the Apple ecosystem is one of the company's defining advantages—it allows for greater optimization and smoother performance, as the AI tools are designed specifically to work with Apple's devices and operating systems. This consistency can lead to a more polished, cohesive user experience, free from the fragmentation that plagues open ecosystems like Android.

However, this closed system can also limit the scope of innovation. In an open ecosystem, developers can freely create and test AI-driven applications, often leading to more rapid experimentation and evolution of new features. By contrast, Apple's closed approach means that AI development is tightly controlled, with fewer opportunities for third-party developers to introduce fresh ideas or push boundaries. While Apple's controlled ecosystem ensures high-quality, secure products, it also means that the company is less nimble than its competitors, such as Google or Microsoft, who are able to iterate on their AI products more quickly by leveraging the vast, open-ended nature of their platforms.

Apple's cautious, privacy-first approach is undeniably strategic, especially in a time when data security and user privacy are at the forefront of tech industry concerns. The company has built its reputation on protecting user data, offering privacy-focused features like on-device processing, secure facial recognition, and end-to-end encryption. In the context of AI, this stance means that Apple's AI tools prioritize user control and privacy, processing as much data on the device as possible rather than sending it to the cloud. This ensures that users' information is protected and that their personal data is not used to fuel AI systems in ways that could compromise their privacy.

But this focus on privacy comes with trade-offs. Because Apple processes data on the device, rather than relying on cloud-based AI models, the company is limited by the processing power of its hardware. This can sometimes result in slower or less sophisticated AI features compared to those of Google or Microsoft, which leverage cloud-based machine learning models and vast data resources to provide more real-time, data-driven insights. For Apple, this is a strategic choice, one that prioritizes user trust over raw AI power. But as AI continues to evolve and become more data-hungry, it remains to be seen whether this approach will be enough to keep pace with competitors who are willing to take more risks with user data in exchange for faster, more powerful AI capabilities.

In the end, Apple's approach to AI is a balancing act between providing a seamless, high-quality user experience and maintaining the privacy and security that its customers expect. Whether this conservative, privacy-driven philosophy will prove to be an advantage or a hindrance in the long term depends on how quickly Apple can innovate within its controlled ecosystem without compromising on its core values.

The delays in rolling out *Apple Intelligence* and the absence of promised features have raised important questions about Apple's broader AI strategy. At the heart of the issue is whether these delays are a result of Apple's cautious approach to innovation or a deeper flaw in its ability to execute on its ambitious promises. The tech community and consumers alike are starting to wonder if Apple, a company that has long been known for pushing the boundaries of design and user experience, is faltering in the race to bring truly transformative AI features to its devices.

From the outset, Apple's AI vision was grand. The company promised a seamless integration of AI tools across its entire ecosystem—from iPhones and iPads to the Vision Pro. The hype around these features was massive, with Apple positioning *Apple Intelligence* as the next big leap in its product evolution. But as the months have rolled by, it's become evident that Apple has not been able to deliver on these promises in a timely fashion. Users who expected groundbreaking changes have instead been met with incremental updates, many of which fall short of their expectations.

The delayed rollout suggests a couple of things about Apple's strategy. On the one hand, it could indicate a commitment to quality. Apple is notoriously careful about its product releases, often taking the time to ensure that features work flawlessly before they're launched. This attention to detail is part of why Apple devices are so beloved by their users—the company's products are designed to be reliable and user-friendly. However, when it comes to AI, this cautious approach has become a double-edged sword. The tech world is moving at a rapid pace, with competitors like Google and Microsoft releasing AI innovations at breakneck speed. By taking its time, Apple risks falling behind, especially as its rivals continue to refine and expand their AI capabilities at a faster rate.

On the other hand, the delays could also point to deeper technical or strategic challenges. AI is a highly complex field, and integrating sophisticated machine learning models into a vast ecosystem like Apple's presents unique obstacles. Apple's decision to prioritize privacy, with an emphasis on on-device processing rather than cloud-based AI, may also be a factor in the delays. While this focus on privacy is a key differentiator for Apple, it also means that AI tools must be built from the ground up to run efficiently on a wide range of devices, without compromising user data or performance. This requires extensive testing and refinement, which can slow down the rollout process.

Despite these challenges, the extended timeline for completing *Apple Intelligence* features raises a crucial question: Is Apple simply taking a more conservative approach, or is it struggling to meet the hype it generated? While there's no doubt that Apple is committed to delivering high-quality, secure AI experiences, there's also a sense that the company may have over-promised and under-delivered. The initial excitement over *Apple Intelligence* has begun to fade as users realize that the transformative features they were promised are taking longer to materialize. As competitors continue to push the envelope in AI innovation, Apple's ability to meet the expectations it set in 2024 will be crucial in determining whether it can maintain its leadership in the tech industry or fall behind in the AI race.

# Chapter 6: What's Missing in Apple Intelligence – The Roadblocks

One of the most glaring issues with *Apple Intelligence* is the absence of some of the core features that were initially promised or expected. While Apple has introduced several AI tools, many of the more advanced capabilities that users were hoping for remain conspicuously absent, creating a sense of disappointment among both casual consumers and professional users alike. These gaps highlight not just the limits of the current rollout but also the challenges Apple faces in trying to truly integrate AI into its entire ecosystem.

## The Lack of AI-Driven Automation Across Devices

One of the most anticipated features of *Apple Intelligence* was the promise of deeper AI-driven automation. Users were excited about the idea of a fully connected Apple ecosystem where devices could predict their needs, offer helpful suggestions, and seamlessly automate routine tasks. Imagine a world where your iPhone, iPad, Mac, and even Apple Watch could work together more intelligently—anticipating which apps you might need, optimizing your device's settings, or even suggesting actions based on your preferences and behavior.

However, despite the hype, *Apple Intelligence* has yet to deliver a truly robust, cross-device AI automation system. While there are some predictive features—like reminders and suggested actions—these are still relatively basic compared to what users were hoping for. The AI feels more reactive than proactive, with many devices still relying on users to manually initiate most actions. For example, while macOS and iOS offer some level of automation through features like Shortcuts, these systems still require a considerable amount of user input to set up and optimize. The kind of intelligent, cross-device orchestration that many users envisioned has yet to fully materialize, leaving a significant gap in the user experience.

## Limited Integration with the Vision Pro

Perhaps the most surprising omission has been the lack of deep AI integration with the Vision Pro, Apple's flagship augmented reality headset. When the Vision Pro was first announced, it was marketed as the future of computing, blending the physical and digital worlds in an immersive experience powered by cutting-edge technology. The AI tools that Apple introduced with *Apple Intelligence* were expected to elevate the Vision Pro into a truly next-generation device, offering intelligent features like context-aware assistants, real-time content creation, and personalized interactions that could transform how users interact with the AR world.

Yet, despite these promises, the Vision Pro has largely been devoid of the AI-powered enhancements that were expected. While the headset does feature some basic AI capabilities, such as eye-tracking and facial recognition, these are far from the robust AI tools that were initially promised. Instead, users have found that the Vision Pro feels more like a highly advanced hardware showcase, with limited software functionality to match its potential. The absence of deeper AI integration in the Vision Pro is a significant missed opportunity, especially as competitors in the AR and VR space are integrating more sophisticated AI features into their own devices. As a result, the Vision Pro's full potential remains untapped, and Apple has yet to deliver on its vision of a truly AI-powered AR experience.

## **The Gap for Professional Creators**

Another area where *Apple Intelligence* has yet to make significant strides is in its support for professional creators, including video editors, developers, and other power users who rely on their devices for high-level creative work. While Apple has made some attempts to integrate AI features into creative tools—like writing assistance and photo editing—these features are still rudimentary and often feel more like basic enhancements than groundbreaking tools.

For video editors, developers, and other professionals who demand highly specialized AI tools, Apple's current offerings are simply not enough. The lack of more advanced AI-driven automation in professional-grade software is a notable gap. For instance, AI tools in programs like Final Cut Pro or Logic Pro are limited, and there's a noticeable absence of sophisticated features like real-time, AI-powered video editing, automatic code generation, or machine learning models that can enhance design workflows. Creative professionals have come to expect AI-driven capabilities in tools like Adobe Premiere Pro or in the growing suite of AI offerings from companies like Microsoft and Google. By not fully integrating AI into its professional software, Apple risks alienating its most demanding user base, who may look elsewhere for the next generation of intelligent, productivity-enhancing tools.

In short, while *Apple Intelligence* shows promise, the lack of core features like deep automation across devices, full integration with the Vision Pro, and advanced AI tools for professional creators leaves many users feeling as though Apple is missing the mark. These absences not only highlight the challenges Apple faces in AI development but also underscore the growing gap between Apple's vision and the industry's current AI capabilities. The question now is whether Apple will be able to close these gaps in time to meet user expectations—or if the company will continue to fall behind its competitors in the race for AI dominance.

In hindsight, while Apple's *Apple Intelligence* rollout has undoubtedly been a significant step forward for the company, there's no doubt that there were missed opportunities that could have made the AI experience more impactful and groundbreaking. Apple has always prided itself on innovation, but when it comes to AI, it seems the company took a more cautious, measured approach. In some ways, this is understandable—Apple is known for not rushing its products to market—but when compared to its competitors, it's clear that Apple could have pushed the envelope further. There were key areas where deeper integration of AI could have made its rollout much more compelling, especially across the wider range of Apple's hardware lineup.

One of the most obvious missed opportunities is the lack of AI integration in Apple's wearables, particularly the Apple Watch. The Apple Watch is one of the company's flagship devices, and it's poised to play a pivotal role in the future of personal health technology. While the watch is excellent at tracking basic metrics like heart rate, calories burned, and sleep patterns, it could have been so much more. Imagine if the watch could intelligently predict health trends, offer customized fitness plans based on the user's past activities, or even alert users about potential health risks based on AI-powered insights. Apple could have integrated more sophisticated AI models to analyze the wearer's health data, predict changes in fitness needs, or provide proactive guidance. This would have set the Apple Watch apart as not just a health tracker but a personalized, intelligent health assistant.

In the same vein, the Apple Watch could have benefited from more AI-driven features around personal productivity and time management. Rather than simply reminding users of scheduled appointments, the watch could have anticipated when a user might need a break, suggested optimal work intervals based on the user's habits, or even recommended focus exercises based on stress levels. The idea of an intelligent wearable that adapts to and learns from a user's behavior is still somewhat underexplored in Apple's current approach.

Another area where Apple could have made a bigger impact with AI is its macOS ecosystem. The Mac has always been the powerhouse for creative professionals—designers, video editors, writers, and developers. Yet, the current iteration of *Apple Intelligence* lacks significant AI tools for these users. There is a clear opportunity here to develop AI-powered tools that could assist with more advanced tasks, such as automating repetitive workflows, enhancing creative projects with smart suggestions, or even helping developers write more efficient code. While Apple has introduced some AI-driven features, like photo recognition and content suggestions, it has not yet tapped into the potential of AI for high-level creative or professional use. By expanding AI tools to better serve the professional and creative sectors, Apple could have not only increased the utility of macOS but also attracted more power users who might otherwise look to other platforms with more comprehensive AI support.

Additionally, Apple's focus on a "closed ecosystem" has its merits in terms of privacy and security, but it also restricts the integration of AI across the broader tech landscape. Unlike Google and Microsoft, which have heavily invested in cloud-based AI platforms that can connect to a wide array of devices and services, Apple's approach to AI remains more self-contained. This approach limits the ability of Apple's AI to be truly cross-platform or adaptable to third-party applications. While Apple's focus on privacy ensures user data stays secure and local, it also prevents Apple Intelligence from being as dynamic as the more open systems offered by competitors.

Ultimately, Apple's cautious, incremental rollout of AI tools has been a double-edged sword. On the one hand, it ensures that features are refined and don't disrupt the user experience. On the other hand, it has led to a feeling of missed potential—where users expected a deeper, more profound integration of AI across the entire Apple ecosystem, they have instead received a more limited set of features that don't quite match the hype. While Apple may be focusing on gradual, stable development, it's clear that the company has the opportunity to push the boundaries of AI in ways that would make its rollout truly revolutionary—especially with more ambitious integration into devices like wearables, macOS, and even the HomePod or Apple TV.

## Chapter 7: The Transformation Ahead – What We Can Expect in 2025 and Beyond

Looking ahead to 2025, the trajectory of Apple's AI strategy holds significant potential to reshape not just the company's product lineup but also the very way we interact with technology on a daily basis. Apple's ambitious plans for *Apple Intelligence* are far from over, and the next few years could see AI evolve from a set of useful tools to an integrated, central part of the Apple ecosystem. The direction Apple takes with its AI rollout will be critical—not just for the company's market position but also for the broader tech landscape, where innovation is happening at lightning speed.

As Apple moves into 2025, its AI capabilities are expected to be more seamlessly woven into its devices, creating a more intelligent and intuitive experience across all its platforms. In fact, AI may soon be the key driver of innovation in the Apple ecosystem. Devices like the iPhone, iPad, Mac, and the Vision Pro, which are already deeply integrated into users' daily lives, will likely evolve into even smarter, more predictive systems. Imagine an iPhone that knows exactly when you need directions, when to remind you of an important email, or when to adjust your device settings based on environmental factors like time of day or location. This type of predictive and anticipatory AI could create a truly personalized experience for users, where their devices seem to "think" ahead and take action before the user even asks.

For example, the iPad and Mac could become even more powerful work tools, integrating AI to assist with more advanced creative tasks. AI-driven content creation, from writing and design to video editing, could be fine-tuned to individual user preferences, streamlining workflows and giving creators more time to focus on the big picture rather than the technical details. Imagine a Mac that intelligently curates your work day, sorting through emails, organizing files, and even making suggestions on how to optimize your workflow based on previous habits. With AI seamlessly integrated, it could feel as if your Mac or iPad is working *with* you rather than just for you.

Beyond the core devices, Apple's wearables, like the Apple Watch and the AirPods, are poised to undergo a major transformation, too. AI could open up new possibilities in health monitoring and personalization. For instance, future versions of the Apple Watch could offer a more sophisticated understanding of user health, beyond just tracking activity or measuring heart rate. With AI, the watch could predict health patterns, offer preventative advice, and even detect early signs of medical issues before they become problems. Coupled with deeper machine learning algorithms, the watch might one day serve as a personal health assistant, offering tailored fitness advice, nutrition tips, or even stress management techniques in real-time.

However, it's not just about improving existing products—it's about creating entirely new ways to interact with technology. Apple's Vision Pro, which is still in its early stages, could be where the most radical AI developments happen. With its augmented reality capabilities, the Vision Pro has the potential to transform how we experience the digital world. AI could help power more natural interactions within this immersive environment, allowing users to control and interact with their virtual world using just their voice, gestures, or even thoughts, as the technology advances. It's a vision that could lead to completely new types of apps, services, and experiences that blur the line between the digital and physical worlds. In this way, Apple's AI could redefine what it means to "use" technology altogether, making interactions smoother, more intuitive, and even more human.

In the next few years, we'll likely see Apple use AI to shape a world where devices don't just respond to commands but anticipate needs and provide assistance even before a user knows they need it. It's a bold vision that, if fully realized, could change everything about the way we interact with technology—creating more efficient, personalized, and seamless experiences for users at every level. From entertainment to productivity, healthcare to education, the future of Apple's AI will be about reshaping the user experience in profound ways that make devices smarter, more intuitive, and more embedded into daily life. But as with all of Apple's most transformative innovations, it will take time, refinement, and strategic decision-making to make that vision a reality.

The integration of AI into Apple's ecosystem has the potential to dramatically change the lives of consumers in ways that go beyond simple automation. As AI becomes more deeply embedded into Apple's devices, it will likely transform how users interact with technology on a daily basis, offering tangible improvements in productivity, creativity, and convenience.

For consumers, AI promises to simplify many aspects of daily life. Tasks that once felt tedious or repetitive—like sorting through emails, managing calendars, or organizing files—will be handled by AI in ways that feel seamless and effortless. The experience of using an iPhone or Mac will evolve from being a series of isolated interactions to a fluid, intelligent exchange with the device. As AI tools become more sophisticated, they will anticipate user needs, offering smart suggestions or automating routine tasks, which will save users precious time. For example, an AI assistant on the iPhone could suggest an optimal time to leave for an appointment based on real-time traffic data, while also reminding you of any last-minute to-dos. On a Mac, AI could analyze your workload and suggest the most efficient way to complete a project based on your past work habits, helping you prioritize tasks in a way that increases overall productivity.

The impact on creativity will be even more profound. Creative professionals, from writers and designers to video editors and musicians, will benefit from tools that help them craft more compelling content with less effort. Generative AI will become a valuable collaborator, whether it's assisting with brainstorming, refining ideas, or producing drafts of written content. On iPads and Macs, AI-powered design tools will assist in the creative process, offering suggestions for layouts, color schemes, or even music composition based on the artist's preferences. With AI taking care of the repetitive and technical tasks, creators will be able to focus on what truly matters: their vision. This will not only enhance productivity but also lower the barrier to entry for aspiring creatives, empowering more people to pursue their passions and produce high-quality work.

For the everyday consumer, the convenience of AI-powered assistants will be a game changer. In the near future, your iPhone or iPad could become an even more indispensable tool for personal and professional life. AI could track habits and preferences, anticipating your needs before you even ask. From automatically adjusting settings based on your location or the time of day to streamlining the shopping experience, AI will be able to offer solutions that feel personalized and efficient.

On a broader scale, Apple's AI ambitions could help revolutionize the entire tech landscape. The company has always been a trendsetter, influencing how people use technology and setting standards that the rest of the industry often follows. As Apple pushes the boundaries of what's possible with AI, it could set a new benchmark for how software and hardware interact, and how they work together to provide a more holistic, intelligent user experience. The promise of AI is not just in making devices smarter, but in transforming the very way we interact with technology itself. Apple's vision for AI is one of deeper integration, where the hardware doesn't just serve as a platform for apps but becomes an active, intelligent partner in the user's daily life. The possibilities for both software and hardware are immense: imagine Apple designing

AI-specific chips that make real-time processing more powerful and efficient, or creating a unified AI system that operates across all Apple devices, from wearables to desktops.

Furthermore, Apple's push to innovate in AI could lead to significant advancements in areas like augmented reality (AR) and virtual reality (VR), especially with the Vision Pro. If Apple succeeds in integrating AI into AR/VR experiences, it could lead to an entirely new way of interacting with the digital world. Users could experience immersive environments that are not only interactive but also adaptive, with AI-driven avatars, virtual assistants, and predictive features that enhance the overall experience. The integration of AI with AR and VR could be the next frontier in digital interaction, potentially revolutionizing industries from gaming to healthcare, education, and beyond.

In all, Apple's AI journey is about more than just adding new features; it's about reimagining what devices can do and how they can serve the user. If

Apple succeeds in fulfilling the promise of its AI strategy, it will not only redefine its own ecosystem but could also reshape the broader tech landscape, pushing the boundaries of what's possible in both hardware and software.

# Chapter 8: The Verdict – Hype or Reality?

As we look at *Apple Intelligence* so far, it's clear that the journey has been one of both promise and underachievement. Apple's bold vision for AI across its product lineup has certainly captured the tech world's attention, but the execution—though impressive in certain aspects—has yet to fully meet the expectations set during its initial announcements. The question on the table now is whether Apple is truly delivering on its promise, or if the AI tools that are slowly rolling out are merely scratching the surface of what could be.

On the one hand, Apple has certainly made strides in its AI integration. The writing tools, predictive features, and some of the automation provided in iOS, macOS, and iPadOS show that Apple is serious about incorporating AI into its products. These features, even in their nascent form, have proven to be valuable to users who appreciate Apple's emphasis on simplicity and ease of use. In particular, the AI-powered writing tools and the integration of predictive capabilities across devices are promising steps in the right direction. They are exactly the type of tools that could improve everyday productivity and creativity for millions of Apple users, making tasks easier and more intuitive.

However, when you look at the bigger picture, there's still a lot left to be desired. The integration of AI is far from comprehensive, and several key features that were promised are still missing. The most glaring omission has been the lack of AI-driven automation across devices. While predictive features exist, they are not as robust or transformative as they could be. Similarly, the lack of AI integration in Apple's flagship Vision Pro headset and wearables like the Apple Watch has left many wondering whether Apple is truly leveraging its AI capabilities to their fullest potential. These devices, which were touted as the next frontiers in personal computing, have yet to see the type of AI-powered evolution many users had hoped for.

When we take a step back and evaluate the timeline, the delayed rollout of features further compounds the feeling of unrealized potential. Apple's promise to have *Apple Intelligence* fully integrated across its ecosystem by March 2025 seems ambitious, but given the pace of development so far, it remains uncertain whether the company can deliver on these high expectations. While Apple's cautious approach to releasing features is often a strength—ensuring quality and reliability—it also risks losing ground to faster-moving competitors who are already rolling out AI features at a quicker pace.

The long-term potential of *Apple Intelligence* remains intriguing, however. If Apple can maintain its focus on quality and privacy while scaling up its AI capabilities, the company could very well redefine how users interact with technology. Apple's commitment to creating a seamless, user-centric experience could lead to AI tools that are not just intelligent but also intuitive, deeply integrated into everyday life in a way that other companies have yet to achieve. But this will only happen if Apple can overcome its current challenges—delivering on its promises in a timely manner, refining its predictive features, and integrating AI across more of its devices.

Ultimately, *Apple Intelligence* has the potential to be a game-changer. But whether it becomes one depends on how Apple addresses the shortcomings of its current rollout. If the company can push past the current gaps in its offerings, *Apple Intelligence* could revolutionize not just its product lineup but the broader tech landscape, setting a new standard for what AI can achieve. If, however, these delays continue and the promises remain half-delivered, *Apple Intelligence* might be remembered as a missed opportunity—an example of great potential that failed to live up to the hype. Only time will tell.

# Conclusion

As we reach the conclusion of this journey through *Apple Intelligence*, it's clear that we're standing on the precipice of something transformative. The excitement that surrounded Apple's announcement of AI-powered features at WWDC 2024 has not entirely dissipated, but the reality of the gradual rollout has tempered expectations. While Apple has introduced several promising AI tools, the full vision of an interconnected, intelligent ecosystem is still unfolding. This is not an end, but rather a pause in what is bound to be a longer journey toward revolutionizing how we interact with our devices.

Looking back, it's evident that Apple's cautious and deliberate approach has shaped the way *Apple Intelligence* has evolved. The company's focus on quality, user experience, and privacy has always set it apart from the competition. Yet, in the fast-moving world of AI, this deliberate pace has meant that some of the promised features have arrived slowly, with gaps in integration and missed opportunities. There's no denying the potential of Apple's AI, but it's clear that the road ahead will require more than just incremental updates—it will require bold, transformative changes that push the boundaries of what's possible.

As the tech world continues to evolve, Apple's AI journey is far from over. While the current state of affairs may seem like a work in progress, the foundation has been laid for a future that could change everything from the way we work to the way we experience the world through technology. With major updates expected by March 2025 and even greater advancements on the horizon, there's every reason to believe that Apple's AI evolution will continue to surprise us.

For those who are invested in Apple's ecosystem, the message is clear: stay tuned. The next chapter is just beginning, and Apple's AI future is still full of possibilities. Whether the company will rise to the occasion and deliver on its full promise remains to be seen, but one thing is certain—the wait will be worth it.